P9-BIT-961

DAILY REFLECTIONS FOR
lent 2010

DANIEL J. HARRINGTON, s.j.

ST. ANTHONY MESSENGER PRESS
Cincinnati, Ohio

RESCRIPT

In accord with the *Code of Canon Law,* I hereby grant my permission to publish
Daily Reflections for Lent 2010, by Daniel J. Harrington.

Reverend Joseph R. Binzer
Vicar General
Archdiocese of Cincinnati
Cincinnati, Ohio
April 17, 2009

The permission to publish is a declaration that a book or pamphlet is considered
to be free from doctrinal or moral error. It is not implied that those who have
granted the permission to publish agree with the contents, opinions or statements expressed.

Cover and book design by Mark Sullivan
Cover image © istockphoto.com/Jaroslaw Baczewski

ISBN 978-0-86716-926-3

Published by St. Anthony Messenger Press
28 W. Liberty St.
Cincinnati, OH 45202
www.SAMPBooks.org

Printed in the United States of America.

Printed on acid-free paper.

10 11 12 13   5 4 3 2 1

Introduction

This booklet presents brief reflections on the Scripture passages read at the Masses each day during Lent of 2010. In cases where the readings for a special feast (February 22, March 19 and 25) replace the lenten texts for the day, I have treated both sets of readings.

For each day I identify a theme that ties together the various biblical texts, suggest a sample prayer (often using words from the Responsorial Psalm for the day) and offer questions that might stimulate thought and prayer. The method employed here is a version of *lectio divina* ("sacred reading"), a practice rooted in Christian monastic history and recently used more widely in personal and pastoral settings. It involves careful reading of a biblical text and analysis of it (What does the text say?), meditation (What does the text say to me?), prayer (What do I want to say to God on the basis of this text?) and action (What should I do in light of this text?).

My hope is that this booklet may illustrate again during Lent of 2010 that "the word of God is living and active, sharper than any two-edged sword" (Hebrews 4:12).

Daniel J. Harrington, S.J.

· · · | · · ·
Be Reconciled to God Now

Ash Wednesday • February 17
JOEL 2:12–18; PSALM 51:3–6, 12–14, 17; 2 CORINTHIANS 5:20—6:2;
MATTHEW 6:1–6, 16–18

On the first day of Lent I often feel a bit hypocritical as I walk around with ashes on my forehead. I keep replaying the Gospel text for Ash Wednesday, in which Jesus warns against performing acts of piety—almsgiving, prayer and fasting—publicly in order to be noticed by others.

Lent is, of course, the traditional time for engaging in these religious practices. The key is to strike a balance between external and internal and to undertake these practices in the proper spirit. Ever the wise teacher, Jesus reminds us to be clear about why we do what we do. Our acts of piety must be part of our reconciliation to, and service of, God, not merely ways of building up a good public image.

In the Old Testament there is only one obligatory fast day, the Day of Atonement (Yom Kippur). However, public fasts could be proclaimed in times of crisis (as in the book of Joel). While neither Joel nor Paul was speaking directly about Lent, what they wrote is especially applicable to Ash Wednesday. Joel insists that "now" is the time to return to God (Joel 2:12). And Paul asserts that "now is the acceptable time" to be reconciled to God (2 Corinthians 6:2). Lent is an opportunity to be reconciled with God, others and ourselves. Jesus has made this kind of reconciliation possible.

Pray

Have mercy on me, O God,
    according to your steadfast love;
according to your abundant mercy
    blot out my transgressions.
Wash me thoroughly from my iniquity,
    and cleanse me from my sin. (Psalm 51:1–2)

Reflect

Do you now feel in need of reconciliation with God or someone else? Is what you are doing for Lent related to this need? Why are you doing it, and what do you hope from it?

• • • | • • •

Choose Life

February 18 • Thursday After Ash Wednesday
Deuteronomy 30:15–20; Psalm 1:1–4, 6; Luke 9:22—25

On the second day of Lent, we are given a choice between the way of life and the way of death. Which will you choose?

In his last great speech, as ancient Israel prepares to enter the Promised Land, Moses places before the people a choice between the way of life and the way of death. The way of life demands keeping God's commandments, and it promises happiness and fullness of life on earth. The way of death involves turning away from God and going astray, and it ends in unhappiness and death. The decision seems easy: Choose life.

Psalm 1 brings the same "two ways" perspective to the entire collection of 150 Psalms. Those who find joy in God's law and take it as their guide in life will prosper while those who follow the counsel of the wicked face ruin. Again the decision seems easy.

But the choice in the Gospel reading is not so simple. Before setting out on his final journey up to Jerusalem, Jesus, according to Luke 9, confronts his disciples with the suffering that he will undergo and the suffering that his disciples can expect to face. Now the decision is not so easy. Now you must take account of the mystery of the cross if you hope to enjoy eternal life and the fullness of God's kingdom. Will you choose life on these terms?

Pray

Lord Jesus, help me to choose life even when it involves suffering, to be true to your teachings even when it is hard to do so and to follow your example with fidelity and courage in the hope of eternal life with you. Amen.

Reflect

What comes to mind when you hear, "Choose life"? Do you take account of the mystery of the cross? What does "life" mean for you in this context?

• • • | • • •

An Acceptable Fast

February 19 • Friday After Ash Wednesday
Isaiah 58:1–9a; Psalm 51:3–6, 18–19; Matthew 9:14–15

Catholics are expected to abstain from meat on Fridays in Lent and to fast on Ash Wednesday and Good Friday. These practices are small reminders of Lent as a special time, and their minor inconvenience can remind us of our participation in Christ's sufferings.

Today's reading from the first half of Isaiah 58 reflects the period after Israel's return from the Babylonian exile, when things were not going well. A public fast was proclaimed in the hope of changing the situation, but the results were disappointing. The people protested that God was not paying attention to their plight.

In response the prophet insisted that their ritual fasting was not enough. For their fortunes to change, they needed to reform their whole society by freeing the oppressed, feeding the hungry and clothing the naked. Likewise, the psalmist contends that the sacrifice God really wants is "a broken and contrite heart" (Psalm 51:17).

Jesus' contemporaries were surprised that his disciples did not engage in devotional fasts as John's disciples and the Pharisees did. In reply Jesus points to his presence as a special time (like a wedding), and so fasting was not appropriate. However, he does envision fasting after his death and Resurrection. And he surely agreed with the prophet that by itself fasting is not enough to force God's hand. Much more is expected of us.

Pray

Lord God, help us during Lent to approach you with humility and respect. May our lenten practices be carried out in the proper spirit of reverence for you and for the good of those in need. Amen.

Reflect

Do you observe the church's program of fasting and abstaining during Lent? Why do you do it, and what do you hope from it? Does it ever prompt you to work for social justice?

• • • | • • •

Divine Help

February 20 • Saturday After Ash Wednesday
Isaiah 58:9b–14; Psalm 86:1–6; Luke 5:27–32

Do you believe that God loves and cares for you, even in your darkest moments? Today's readings remind us that God wants to help turn our lives around, is eager to hear our prayers and delights in our good deeds.

The attention that Jesus paid to religiously and socially marginal persons surprised his contemporaries. Tax collectors were suspected of dishonesty and political disloyalty. Sinners were those who by their lifestyle or occupation failed to observe the Mosaic Law. Jesus defended his ministry to such persons since they had the most need of his help. If Jesus could bring God's love and care to those disreputable persons, surely he can do so for us.

Psalm 86 is a plea for divine help in what seemed like a desperate situation. The psalmist recognizes his need for help ("I am poor and needy") and throws himself on God's mercy (v. 1). When we make the psalmist's words our own, we are letting God help in turning our lives around.

The second half of Isaiah 58 challenges us to work for a just society by struggling against oppression and tending to those in need. It also insists on observing the Sabbath as a witness to God's work of creation and our human need for rest. When we let God help shape our lives, we can help others and approach God in peace and joy.

Pray

For you, O Lord, are good and forgiving,
 abounding in steadfast love to all who call
  on you.
Give ear, O LORD, to my prayer;
 listen to my cry of supplication.
 (Psalm 86:5–6)

Reflect

Are there areas in your life where you need God's help? Have you talked about it with God and with your loved ones? What might help you most?

· · · | · · ·

Resisting Temptation

February 21 • The First Sunday of Lent
Deuteronomy 26:4–10; Psalm 91:1–2, 10–15;
Romans 10:8–13; Luke 4:1–13

On the first Sunday of Lent it is customary to read a Gospel account about the temptation of Jesus. The episode clarifies what kind of Son of God Jesus is before he begins his public ministry. It also challenges us to examine what kind of Christians we are.

According to Luke, Jesus had spent, under the Holy Spirit's initiative, forty days in the wilderness engaged in prayer and fasting. His experience provides the biblical model for the lenten season. At the end of this period, Jesus enters into a scriptural debate with the devil.

The three temptations, or tests, concern physical comfort, political power and spectacular display. At each point Jesus rejects the devil's offer with a quotation from Deuteronomy 6—8. Thus he proves his total dedication to his heavenly Father and the Word of God. As the faithful Son of God, Jesus passes the tests that the wilderness generation of ancient Israel had failed.

Jesus may well have faced the three temptations described in this episode throughout his public ministry. Indeed, desires for pleasure, power and fame are temptations that face most of us in some form or other. Jesus provides us with a positive example of resistance to such temptation and victory over them. As God's faithful Son, he serves God alone and lives in harmony with God's Word.

Pray

Heavenly Father, be my shelter, refuge and stronghold in all the tests and temptations that life brings me. Answer me when I call upon you, and deliver me from the snares of the devil. Amen.

Reflect

In what areas of life do you feel tested or tempted? How do you deal with these temptations? How might you work on these temptations during this Lent?

· · · | · · ·

Peter, the Forgiven Sinner

February 22 • The Chair of Saint Peter, Apostle
1 PETER 5:1–4; PSALM 23:1–6; MATTHEW 16:13–19

The readings for the "Chair of Saint Peter" replace the usual lenten texts for the first Monday of Lent. Today's liturgy is both a memorial of Peter and a celebration of the papacy. The Latin word for "chair" or "seat" is *sedes,* the term underlying the expression "the Holy See" with reference to the papacy. The Catholic Church traces the institution of the papacy back to Peter as the first bishop of Rome. As the bishop of Rome, the pope is thus regarded as the successor of Peter.

In Matthew Jesus blesses Peter as the recipient of a divine revelation because he confessed Jesus to be "the Messiah, the Son of the living God" (16:16). He goes on to appoint Peter as the "rock" (a play on Peter's name) on which the church is to be built, and a strong force who is capable of exercising divine authority. In 1 Peter 5, Peter identifies himself as a presbyter and witness to the suffering of Christ.

The celebration of this feast during Lent reminds us of another dimension of Peter—the forgiven sinner. Each of the Gospels tells us that on the eve of Jesus' death Peter denied even knowing Jesus. Nevertheless, the Risen Jesus pardoned Peter (see especially John 21) and restored him to his position of preeminence among the first disciples. If God was willing to forgive Peter, how much more is God willing to forgive whatever sins we may have committed.

Pray

Lord God, we thank you for giving us the example of Peter, the forgiven sinner, and we ask that you show the same kind of mercy to us for our sins. Amen.

Reflect

Why did Peter deny knowing Jesus? How do you explain Peter's transformation after Easter? In what sense is the pope the successor of Peter?

• • • | • • •

How to Love Your Neighbor

February 22 • Monday of the First Week of Lent
LEVITICUS 19:1–2, 11–18; PSALM 19:8–10, 15;
MATTHEW 25:31–46

Today's Old Testament reading ends with a commandment that Jesus made into an essential element of his teaching, "You shall love your neighbor as yourself"

(Leviticus 19:18). It is certainly an admirable sentiment. But what does it mean practically?

What we should *not* do to love our neighbor appears in the selection from Leviticus. Part of the "Holiness Code," it challenges ancient Israelites (and us) to reflect on and emulate the holiness of God, "You shall be holy, for I the Lord your God, am holy" (19:2). Most verses in this reading are cast in the form of prohibitions ("You shall not…") and concern dealings with other persons, especially in realms of business, law and social relations. Those who love their neighbor will not steal, or lie, or swear falsely and so on. There are many obvious parallels to the Ten Commandments here.

What we should do to love our neighbor emerges from the great judgment scene in Matthew. In the context of the Last Judgment, "all the nations" are to be rewarded or condemned on the basis of their deeds with respect to their neighbors in need: feeding the hungry, giving drink to the thirsty, welcoming the stranger, clothing the naked, caring for the sick and visiting the imprisoned (25:32). What surprises those being judged is the realization that in performing these compassionate actions they were doing them for Jesus, the glorious Son of Man.

Pray

O Lord, my rock and redeemer, may I always heed your words and keep to your way of wisdom. May my thoughts and actions always find favor before you. Amen.

Reflect

Use the two lists of deeds—those to be avoided and those to be practiced—as material for an examination of conscience. How do you make out? What are your failures, and what are your successes?

· · · | · · ·

God's Words and Our Words
February 23 • Tuesday of the First Week of Lent
Isaiah 55:10–11; Psalm 34:4–7, 16–19; Matthew 6:7–15

During Lent we are exposed to many of the great texts of Scripture, the book that we often call "the Word of God." We also intensify our prayer life, and in doing so we try to speak to God, though we are all too conscious that our words are weak and limited instruments.

However, the Word of God is much more than the words written in the book we call the Bible. In fact, the Bible itself describes the Word of God as active in creation and salvation history, inspiring the prophets and conveying true wisdom. The prophet Isaiah's comparison of

God's Word to the rain and snow coming down upon the earth illustrates beautifully the active and effective dimension of the biblical concept. God's Word does many things. The New Testament insists that while God has spoken in various ways, he has spoken most definitively in Jesus as the Word of God (see John 1:1–18; Hebrews 1:1–4). What God wants to say, he says through Jesus. The Bible is a privileged witness to God's Word.

In prayer we speak words to God. In the Lord's Prayer, or "Our Father," we have the prayer given to us through Jesus, the Word of God. He invites us to address God as "Our Father" and urges us to pray for the fullness of God's kingdom and for sustenance in the present and future as we await that fullness. Our prayers need not be wordy. The only condition is that we be prepared to forgive others as God has forgiven us.

Pray

Father, your Son Jesus has invited us to share in his special relationship with you. You know what we need before we do. Deliver us from our fears that we may glorify you. Amen.

Reflect

How does God speak to you? How do you speak to God? Read the "Our Father" slowly and meditatively, pausing at each phrase and letting God speak to you through it.

• • • | • • •

The Sign of Jonah
February 24 • Wednesday of the First Week of Lent
JONAH 3:1–10; PSALM 51:3–4, 12–13, 18–19;
LUKE 11:29–32

Jonah was a reluctant prophet. His mission was to preach repentance to the people of Nineveh, who were among ancient Israel's fiercest enemies. But he did not want them to repent. Rather, he wanted God to punish them. So instead of going eastward to Nineveh, he tried to go by ship as far west as possible. That is how he got swallowed by the big fish and spat out on dry land.

Jonah learned his lesson and reluctantly took up his prophetic mission of threatening the Ninevites with destruction unless they repented. Much to his disappointment, they took his warning seriously and repented wholeheartedly. So the forgiving and merciful God of Israel relented and did not punish them.

Jesus was a different kind of prophet. He wanted those who seemed to be God's enemies to repent and enjoy God's mercy. In the context of Luke's Gospel, the "sign of Jonah" refers to the amazing success that Jesus the prophet of divine forgiveness and mercy had with the most unlikely members of his society. His disappointment was with those who could and should have repented and refused to do so. Through Jesus the prophet, we, too, can approach God and seek his forgiveness and mercy. If the Ninevites and the tax collectors and sinners could repent and find forgiveness and mercy, so can we.

Pray

Create in me a clean heart, O God,
and put a new and right spirit within me.
Do not cast me away from your presence,
and do not take your holy spirit from me.
(Psalm 51:10–11)

Reflect

Have you examined your conscience recently? For what do you feel the need for God's forgiveness and mercy? Have you been to confession recently?

· · · | · · ·

The Power of Prayer

February 25 • Thursday of the First Week of Lent
Esther C:12, 14–16, 23–25; Psalm 138:1–3, 7–8; Matthew 7:7–12

The Hebrew version of the book of Esther never mentions God and contains no prayers. Rather, it develops an indirect, or implicit, theology in which God works "behind the scenes" to save his people from destruction through Esther and her guardian, Mordecai. To remedy this perceived deficiency, the Greek translators added references to God and Queen Esther's prayer of petition.

No one was allowed (under penalty of death) to approach the Persian king without being invited by him. In order to save her people, Esther had to inform the king about the wicked Haman's plots against the Jews. So in what is a model of the prayer of petition, Esther asks God to guide and protect her in what will be a pivotal step in saving her people.

The Jewish daily prayer was (and is) structured around a series of petitions in which the people beg for divine mercy, guidance and protection. Jesus' instruction about prayers of petition in Matthew 7 stands in the Jewish tradition. What we call the "Lord's Prayer" is a prayer of petition. But Jesus goes beyond his contemporaries by his insistence on the power of petitionary prayer ("Ask, and it will be given you") and in his confidence that his heavenly Father is eager to hear our prayers and to give good things to those who ask him (see Matthew 7:7).

Pray

I give you thanks, O LORD, with my whole
    heart;
  before the gods I sing your praise.
  (Psalm 138:1)

Reflect

For what do you ask God in your prayers? Are your prayers answered? Do you have confidence that they will be answered?

• • • | • • •

Jesus' Better Righteousness

February 26 • Friday of the First Week of Lent
EZEKIEL 18:21–28; PSALM 130:1–8; MATTHEW 5:20–26

To the Jewish exiles in Babylon in the early sixth century BC, the prophet Ezekiel brought both good and bad news. The younger exiles felt doomed because of the sins of their "fathers." They interpreted the exile as punishment for the sins of earlier generations and saw no good future for themselves.

To them Ezekiel offered good news: the concept of individual responsibility and the possibility of personal transformation. Ezekiel's good news was that we can change if we want to do so. A wicked person can turn from sin and walk in the way of virtue and find life. His bad news was that a good person can also turn away from virtue and walk in the way of sin.

While accepting Ezekiel's emphasis on individual responsibility and personal transformation, Jesus challenges us to pursue what is an even better righteousness. That involves going to the roots of the biblical commandments. The biblical commandment says, "You shall not murder" (Matthew 5:21).With his various illustrations in Matthew 5, Jesus urges us to move beyond and behind the letter of the Law and go to the anger that is at the root of murder. And so he challenges us to avoid provocative language ("You fool") and to reconcile as soon as possible with others with whom we may have a dispute (5:22). That, too, is very good news.

Pray

If you, O Lᴏʀᴅ, should mark iniquities,
    Lord, who could stand?
But there is forgiveness with you,
    so that you may be revered.
    (Psalm 130:3–4)

Reflect

Have you ever undergone a moral conversion? What prompted it? Are there aspects of your life now that may need repentance and repair?

• • • | • • •

Imitating God

February 27 • Saturday of the First Week of Lent
Dᴇᴜᴛᴇʀᴏɴᴏᴍʏ 26:16–19; Psᴀʟᴍ 119:1–2, 4–5, 7–8; Mᴀᴛᴛʜᴇᴡ 5:43–48

Covenant is a central biblical concept. In making a covenant or agreement with ancient Israel, God chose them to be a people especially dear to him and promised to remain faithful to them. In return God expected Israel to observe his commandments, or covenant stipulations, as the proper response to his divine initiative.

In both Testaments morality is covenantal, not strictly legalistic. It is a loving response to the special favor (the meaning of grace) shown to us by God. The covenant provides the theological framework for the 613 commandments in the Torah (the first five books of the Hebrew Bible). According to the New Testament, Jesus is the definitive proof of God's covenantal fidelity, and Jesus is the authoritative interpreter of God's Law.

In Matthew 5, Jesus once more challenges us to go beyond the letter of the Law. Moses says, "[L]ove your neighbor" (Leviticus 19:18), but Jesus exhorts us to love even our enemies. In many instances, of course, it is in our own interest to love our neighbor. But to love our enemy goes beyond self-interest. It pushes us into the realm of grace. Jesus bases this teaching on the example of his heavenly Father who cares for all persons, both good and bad. Thus he urges us to look at others from God's perspective and to show the kind of favor (or grace) that God has shown to his chosen people and shows to us through his Son Jesus and the Holy Spirit.

Pray
Lord, may I be faithful in keeping your commandments. Help me to love all my brothers and sisters, even those who do not love me. Amen.

Reflect

Have you ever made a sincere effort to love an enemy? Why did you do it? What happened as a result?

• • • | • • •

High Hopes

February 28 • The Second Sunday of Lent
Genesis 15:5–12, 17–18; Psalm 27:1, 7–9, 13–14; Philippians 3:17—4:1;
Luke 9:28–36

The Gospel text for the Second Sunday of Lent concerns the Transfiguration of Jesus. While pointing to the suffering and death that await Jesus in Jerusalem, the episode also emphasizes as a kind of preview of the glory that the Risen Jesus will enjoy. Thus the episode is sign toward grand or high hopes. According to the New Testament, the three great hopes are right relationship with God, eternal life with God and the fullness of God's kingdom.

The Bible presents us with a gradual escalation and purification of hope. In Genesis 15 Abraham trusts in God's promise of many descendants and the Promised Land and so is declared in right relationship with God. The psalmist hopes to enjoy God's goodness "in the land of the living" (Psalm 27:13), probably a reference to God's presence in the Jerusalem temple. Paul reminds the Philippians that their true home is heaven and urges them to look forward to the second coming of the "Lord Jesus Christ" (Philippians 3:20).

The Transfiguration suggests that Jesus' Passion and death will lead to his exaltation (Resurrection and Ascension) and will bring us to right relationship with God, eternal life with God and the fullness of God's kingdom. At this point in Lent, we are urged to hope on a grand scale—through Jesus' death and Resurrection.

Pray

May the God of hope fill you with all joy and peace in believing, so that you may abound in hope by the power of the Holy Spirit. (Romans 15:13)

Reflect

What do you hope for? Why do you hope? Do you have any "high" hopes?

· · · | · · ·
God, the Merciful One
March 1 · Monday of the Second Week of Lent
Daniel 9:4–10; Psalm 79:8–9, 11, 13; Luke 6:36–38

The two great attributes of God, according to the Bible, are justice and mercy. In most cases mercy overrides or trumps justice.

Much of the book of Daniel deals with conflicts and contests, dreams and visions. Chapter nine, however, is a prayer, a lament over the destruction of Jerusalem and its temple in the early sixth century BC. Daniel traces this catastrophe to the sins of God's people and admits that the exile was just punishment. However, speaking on behalf of the exiles, Daniel appeals to God as the merciful one and to God's compassion and forgiveness.

Psalm 79 begins with a graphic description of the same events and appeals to the "name" of God, that is, the reputation and honor of God. In particular, what is at stake is whether the God of Israel really is the "merciful" one (Luke 6:36).

By his preaching of forgiveness and his healing actions, Jesus made manifest the mercy of God. He helped all kinds of people to turn away from sin and find a new relationship with God. His one condition was that they (and we) "Be merciful, just as your Father is merciful" (Luke 6:36).

Pray

Help us, O God of our salvation,
    for the glory of your name;
deliver us, and forgive our sins,
    for your name's sake. (Psalm 79:9)

Reflect

Do you find a tension between God's justice and God's mercy? Do you pray to God as the merciful one? Does this help you to be more compassionate and merciful to others?

$$\cdots \mid \cdots$$

True Religion

March 2• Tuesday of the Second Week of Lent
Isaiah 1:10, 16–20; Psalm 50: 8–9, 16–17, 21, 23; Matthew 23:1–12

Most people regard the Bible as a "religious" book. But some of the most prominent figures in the Bible—Isaiah, the psalmist and Jesus—promote an understanding of religion that challenges common assumptions about the nature of religion.

The eighth-century BC prophet Isaiah identifies his people and their leaders as Sodom and Gomorrah, biblical cities destroyed for their wickedness. According to Isaiah, true religion involves ceasing to do evil and turning one's life around. It also demands working for justice, illustrated by caring for orphans and widows as the most defenseless members of society.

While not dismissing material sacrifices, Psalm 50 insists on personal integrity and acting upon God's commandments. It also encourages giving thanks and praise to God and approves those who walk in "the right way" (50:23).

In a strong indictment of the religious leaders of time, Jesus insists that true religion must involve practicing what one preaches. It does not consist merely in cultivating a public reputation for being religious. It does consist in the service of others and humility. What better examples of true religion do we have than Isaiah, the psalmist and Jesus?

Pray
Father, help me to understand better how to be truly religious, walk in the right way, practice what I profess and serve others after the example of Jesus, your Son. Amen.

Reflect

How do you define religion? Does your concept fit well with the Bible's concept? What might you need to change in how you understand and practice religion?

• • • | • • •

The Prophet's Burden

March 3 • Wednesday of the Second Week of Lent
JEREMIAH 18:18–20; PSALM 31:5–6, 14–16;
MATTHEW 20:17–28

Being a prophet has never been easy. In biblical times prophets spoke the hard truths that God wished to tell his people. They often challenged their people to turn from comfortable but sinful ways and warned about the bad consequences of not doing so.

Both Jeremiah and Jesus fit the biblical pattern of the prophet. Today's text from Jeremiah 18 describes the hostility he experienced from the citizens of Jerusalem in the late seventh and early sixth centuries BC despite his reliance on God and effort to intercede with God for them. Jeremiah's ultimate allegiance was to the word of God. He was widely misunderstood and rejected. He suffered greatly. That is the burden of the prophet—to proclaim God's truth regardless of the personal cost.

Like Jeremiah, Jesus bore the prophet's burden. On the way to Jerusalem, he foresaw that his journey was going to involve suffering and death. He experienced misunderstanding from his own people and even from his disciples. His concern was not popular opinion, personal comfort or fame. Rather, he came to serve and give his life as "a ransom for many" (Matthew 20:28).

What kept prophets like Jeremiah and Jesus going was the conviction that they were sent by God to proclaim the truth that God's people needed to hear—whether they liked it or not. That is the prophet's burden.

Pray

Into your hand I commit my spirit;
yout have redeemed me, O Lord, faithful God.
(Psalm 31:5)

Reflect

Is there anyone in our time whom you regard as a prophet? What truth does that prophet tell? What has been the result?

· · · | · · ·

A Good Scare

March 4 • Thursday of the Second Week of Lent
Jeremiah 17:5–10; Psalm 1:1–4, 6; Luke 16:19–31

Sometimes we need a good scare. In our world today there is great and growing disparity between rich and poor. Some people live in mansions, while others scavenge in garbage dumps to find food and clothing. There was a similar situation in Jesus' time. His parable of the rich man and Lazarus presupposes that disparity, and so it should scare us today as much as it probably did people two thousand years ago.

The rich man had a lavish lifestyle, while poor Lazarus was sick and reduced to begging. The rich man seems totally unaware of the poor man's existence. He makes no effort to recognize and alleviate the poor man's plight. He remains "blissfully" unaware.

When both men die, their fortunes are reversed. The rich man is confined to what we call hell while poor Lazarus (his name means "God helps") finds himself in "Abraham's bosom," or heaven. The criterion for their judgment seems to have been what was the object of their hope and trust. In the case of Lazarus it was God, whereas for the rich man it was his material possessions.

With God's judgment, the fate of each man is fixed. The message of Jesus' parable is trust in God now, recognize the needs of others now and share your goods with others now—before it is too late.

Pray

Lord, open my eyes, mind and heart to the suffering of the poor in our world today. Give me the courage to act now before it is too late for them and for me. Amen.

Reflect

Does Jesus' parable frighten you? Why? Do you ever give thought to the economic disparities in our world today? Can you do anything about them?

• • • | • • •

Joseph and Jesus

March 5 • Friday of the Second Week of Lent
GENESIS 37:3–4, 12–13, 17–28; PSALM 105:16–21;
MATTHEW 21:33–43, 45–46

The patriarch Joseph appears as the major figure in the last quarter of Genesis. In many respects he is a type, or prefiguration, of Jesus. Both Joseph and Jesus are loved by their fathers, recount dreams and visions about the future, evoke hostility from their kin, suffer persecution from them and eventually save their people.

Genesis 37 tells the story of how the Old Testament Joseph was sold into slavery on account of the envy of his brothers. These men were the sons of Jacob and so the ancestors of the twelve tribes of Israel. Only the intercession of Reuben and Judah prevented Joseph from being killed. Joseph eventually came to Egypt, rose to power and prominence in the Egyptian government and so was able to save his father and brothers from death in the midst of a great famine.

Jesus' parable of the murderous tenant farmers echoes the story of Joseph and prefigures his own Passion and death. It is important to bear in mind that the target of this story was the political and religious leadership (the chief priests and scribes), not Israel as a whole. In fact, the vineyard, which is a symbol of Israel as the people of God (see Isaiah 5:1–7), is not destroyed. What it needed was new and better leadership. Jesus, the servant leader, has provided that.

Pray

Lord God, we thank and praise you for raising up servant leaders like Joseph and Jesus for your people. May we imitate their fidelity and compassion in the midst of misunderstanding and suffering. Amen.

Reflect

Read more about Joseph in Genesis 37—50. How would you describe Joseph? How does he point to Jesus?

• • • | • • •

Who Is the Prodigal One?

March 6 • Saturday of the Second Week of Lent
MICAH 7:14–15, 18–20; PSALM 103:1–4, 9–12;
LUKE 15:1–3, 11–32

One of the features of Jesus' public ministry that disturbed the Pharisees and scribes was the attention that he paid to tax collectors (very likely dishonest and unpatriotic persons) and sinners (Jews who by their occupation or lifestyle did not observe the Law of Moses). Their hostility provides the context for the parable of the Prodigal Son.

The word *prodigal* can refer negatively to someone who spends lavishly and foolishly. That definition fits the younger son. He demands a share of his inheritance, goes off and squanders it and finds that he is penniless and disgraced. Finally he comes to his senses, resolves to turn from his evil ways and goes back to his father's house.

Prodigal can also have a positive sense. That usage fits the father. When he sees his son returning home, he is filled with compassion, welcomes him back and throws a lavish party. Thus he displays the attitude of God, who, according to Micah, is constantly "pardoning iniquity and passing over...transgression" (7:18).

That leaves the older son. While honest and dependable, he resents his brother's foolish prodigality and his father's prodigal display of love. He mirrors the Pharisees and scribes in their resentment over Jesus' ministry to tax collectors and sinners.

Pray

Who is a God like you, pardoning iniquity
  and passing over the transgression of the remnant of
  your possession? (Micah 7:18)

Reflect

Which character in the parable is most like you? Is it the sinful younger son or the forgiving father or the resentful older son? What can you do about it?

• • • | • • •

Justice and Mercy

March 7 • Third Sunday of Lent

EXODUS 3:1–8, 13–15; PSALM 103:1–8, 11;
1 CORINTHIANS 10:1–6, 10–12; LUKE 13:1–9

The God revealed in the Bible is merciful and just. According to Exodus 3, the God who manifested himself to Moses is the God of Abraham, Isaac and Jacob. This same God heard the cries of Israel enslaved in Egypt and promised to lead his people from slavery to freedom. Psalm 103 celebrates the mercy of God and also describes the Lord as the one who secures justice and the rights of the oppressed.

Paul, however, reminds us that not all the Israelites in the exodus generation entered the Promised Land. He notes that most of them were struck down in the desert because of their rebelliousness and sinfulness. The God of the Bible is also just.

Today's passage from Luke 13 brings together the themes of God's justice and mercy. When questioned about two cases of sudden and unexpected deaths, Jesus refuses to be drawn into a debate about personal guilt. Rather, he takes the two cases as warnings to repent and reform in the present, before it is too late. The premise is that God is just and demanding. On the other hand, Jesus' parable about the fig tree that fails to produce fruit reminds us of the patience of God. God never gives up on our repentance and is willing to give us more time. But, God's patience is not completely open-ended.

Pray

The LORD is merciful and gracious,
   slow to anger and abounding in steadfast love.
(Psalm 103:8)

Reflect

How do you relate to God's justice and mercy in your own life? Which do you need most now? Is there anyone close to you whom you wish would repent and reform now?

$$\cdot \ \cdot \ \cdot \ | \ \cdot \ \cdot \ \cdot$$

Prophetic Succession

March 8 · Monday of the Third Week of Lent
2 KINGS 5:1–15; PSALM 42:2–3; 43:3–4; LUKE 4:24–30

Many of Jesus' contemporaries correctly identified him as a prophet. Jesus did what prophets do. He proclaimed God's will to his people, pointed them toward the future fullness of God's kingdom, warned them to turn from sinful ways and performed symbolic actions as a way of teaching.

Of all the Old Testament prophets, Jesus most resembled Elijah and Elisha. Elisha was the disciple and successor of Elijah. The exploits of these prophets are described in fascinating detail from 1 Kings 17 to 2 Kings 9.

The story of Elisha's healing the leprosy of the Syrian general Naaman is typical of the Elijah-Elisha cycle. It is a well-told narrative of God's power at work through the agency of the prophet. What is unusual is that the recipient of God's favor here is a non-Jew. Naaman's confession of faith, however, is among the most memorable and important theological statements in the whole Bible: "Now I know that there is no God in all the earth except in Israel" (2 Kings 5:15).

In Luke 4, Jesus points to Elijah and Elisha as his models. In explaining to his angry neighbors why he was not doing more for them, Jesus points to the ministry of those two great prophets to non-Jews. Thus right from the start of Jesus' public activity, Luke connects Jesus with the two great Israelite prophets who brought the power of the God of Israel to all the nations.

Pray

O send out your light and your truth;
    let them lead me;
let them bring me to your holy hill
    and to your dwelling. (Psalm 43:3)

Reflect

Read more about Elijah and Elisha in the Bible. How would you describe them? What parallels with Jesus do you find? How can the church be more prophetic?

• • • | • • •

Forgive Us Our Trespasses

March 9 • Tuesday of the Third Week of Lent
Daniel 3:25, 34–43; Psalm 25:4–9; Matthew 18:21–35

Every time we recite the "Our Father," we say, "Forgive us our trespasses as we forgive those who trespass against us." That sentence makes a link between our hope for forgiveness from God and our willingness to forgive those who may have sinned against us. Today's readings can help us explore that link in some depth.

The passage from Daniel is part of the Prayer of Azariah that appears in the Greek version of the book. Azariah was one of the three young Jewish men thrown into a fiery furnace for their unwillingness to worship the statue of the Babylonian king. His prayer is a plea for divine forgiveness on behalf of Jews living in exile in Babylon. Azariah approaches God with a "contrite heart and a humble spirit" (3:39). He asks God to forgive the people's sins, which brought on their plight. He appeals to God's kindness and mercy and begs for deliverance. His prayer is answered in a miraculous rescue.

The parable of the unforgiving servant is a dramatizing of the idea that forgiven sinners must forgive those who sin against them. A king forgives the servant a huge debt. But when that servant is unwilling to forgive a fellow servant's smaller debt, the king rescinds his initial forgiveness. The point is that if you wish God to forgive your sins, you must be willing to forgive others.

Pray
Be mindful of your mercy, O LORD, and of your steadfast love,

for they have been from of old.

…

according to your steadfast love remember
    me,
  for your goodness' sake, O Lord.
  (Psalm 25:6,7)

Reflect

Are you asking God for forgiveness? How do you express
that in prayer? Do you need to forgive someone else?

• • • | • • •

Fulfilling the Law and the Prophets
March 10 • Wednesday of the Third Week of Lent
DEUTERONOMY 4:1, 5–9; PSALM 147:12–13, 15–16, 19–20;
MATTHEW 5:17–19

Ancient Israel's identity as God's chosen people was inti-
mately related to its observance of the Law revealed to
Moses on Mount Sinai and written down in the first five
books of the Bible. In his speech to the people, Moses
emphasizes how close the Lord God has been to them and
how wise God's commandments are. He urges them to
teach these things to the coming generations.

    In the Sermon on the Mount, Jesus claims that he has
come "not to abolish but to fulfill" the Law and the
prophets (Matthew 5:17). How does Jesus fulfill the Law

and the prophets? Matthew's Gospel provides several ways of thinking about this question.

In his Infancy and Passion Narratives, Matthew repeatedly shows how Old Testament prophecies were fulfilled by Jesus. The evangelist also connects Jesus with great figures in Israel's history: Abraham, Moses and David. In the Sermon on the Mount, Jesus illustrates how the Law can be more perfectly fulfilled by going to the root of the biblical commandments. For example, if you want to avoid murder, avoid anger, which is the root of murder. In his five great speeches Jesus appears as the authoritative interpreter of the Law. In a real sense Jesus is the embodiment of his people Israel and Emmanuel ("God with us") and so is the goal toward which the Law and prophets pointed.

Pray

Lord God, you have chosen Israel as your special people and proclaimed your word to them. Help us to appreciate more deeply the context in which Jesus as the Word of God lived among us. Amen.

Reflect

Does the Old Testament have a place in your spiritual life? How often do you read it? Does it help you understand Jesus better?

• • • | • • •

Signs of Contradiction

March 11 • Thursday of the Third Week of Lent
JEREMIAH 7:23–28; PSALM 95:1–2, 6–9; LUKE 11:14–23

Many great biblical figures were signs of contradiction. Jeremiah, Moses and Jesus are good examples. On the one hand, they sometimes contradicted popular opinion among their contemporaries. On the other hand, they were often contradicted by the very persons to whom God sent them. Yet they carried on faithfully—out of their allegiance to the call of God.

The prophet Jeremiah tried to lead his fellow Judeans to turn aside from idolatry and moral evils. In Jeremiah's view this was the only way in which they might escape being defeated and destroyed by the Babylonians. But the people would not listen to Jeremiah and accept his word from the Lord.

Psalm 95 reminds us that Moses also was a sign of contradiction. He had led the Hebrews from slavery in Egypt to freedom. Nevertheless, at several points as they made their way through the wilderness, the people rebelled against his leadership and so also God's leadership.

Likewise, Jesus suffered opposition from his contemporaries. In response to his healings and exorcisms, some prominent leaders accused him of being in league with the devil. With a series of short parables, Jesus refuted their charges and affirmed that he was acting out of God's power and that his miracles were in fact signs that "the kingdom of God has come to you" (Luke 11:20).

Pray

O come, let us worship and bow down,
    let us kneel before the Lord, our Maker!
For he is our God,
    and we are the people of his pasture,
    and the sheep of his hand. (Psalm 95:6–7)

Reflect

What enabled and inspired these biblical heroes to carry on? How do you interpret Jesus' miracles? In what sense are they signs of the presence of God's kingdom?

· · · | · · ·

The Three Loves

March 12 · Friday of the Third Week of Lent
HOSEA 14:2–10; PSALM 81:6–11, 14, 17;
MATTHEW 12:28–34

The biblical concept of love has three dimensions: God's love for us, our love for God and our love for one another. Today's readings can help us better understand all three elements.

The prophet Hosea was very much the prophet of God's love for his people. At several points he depicts God as a loving husband and Israel as a wayward wife. God wants nothing more than for her to turn from her evil ways. His love is everlasting. Even though she is unfaithful, God remains faithful to her. For us all, the experience of God's love for us is fundamental. We can rely on God to be steadfast in loving us, just as God showed steadfast love for his people Israel.

When asked to summarize the Law and the prophets, Jesus quoted two commandments among the 613: Love the Lord your God (see Deuteronomy 6:5) and love your neighbor (see Leviticus 19:18). Following the words of Scripture, Jesus insists that our love for God involves every aspect of our being—heart, soul, mind and strength. Then he challenges us to show the same love to others that we so instinctively show to ourselves. Jesus' double love command is based on the conviction that God has loved us first. Loved by God, we can and should love God and love others in return.

Pray

We thank and praise you for the sign of love that you have shown us. Help us to love you in return and to love one another in Jesus' name. Amen.

Reflect

When and how have you experienced God's love for you? Why and how do you show love for God? Does your experience of God's love help you to love others?

• • • | • • •

True Prayer

March 13 • Saturday of the Third Week of Lent
Hosea 6:1–6; Psalm 51:3–4, 18–21; Luke 18:9–14

In Greek mythology Narcissus was a boy who fell in love with his own image in a pool of water. He wasted away because he was unable ever to fulfill his desire. Today we sometimes refer to persons who seem totally self-absorbed as *narcissists*. The parable about the Pharisee and the tax collector reminds us that even spiritual persons can be narcissists.

In Jesus' time the Pharisees were regarded as very serious religious persons. They tried to adapt the Law of Moses to their own circumstances and engaged in communal and individual acts of piety. However, the prayer attributed to the Pharisee in Jesus' parable is more an exercise in self-congratulation than a true prayer.

The Pharisee begins well enough by addressing God and giving thanks. But then with much "I" language he lists his own virtues and religious practices. This is spiritual narcissism, not true prayer.

A better and more authentic prayer comes from the tax collector, someone suspected of dishonesty and political collaboration. He says, "God, be merciful to me, a sinner" (Luke 18:13). His prayer is short and to the point. He recognizes his own weakness and need for divine healing. He calls upon God's mercy and hopes for spiritual renewal. True prayer demands a contrite and humbled heart.

Pray

The sacrifice acceptable to God is a broken spirit;
> a broken and contrite heart, O God, you will not
> despise. (Psalm 51:17)

Reflect

How do you pray? What is the focus of your prayer? To what extent is your prayer "like a morning cloud, / like the dew that goes away early" (Hosea 6:4)?

• • • | • • •

You Can Go Home Again

March 14 • Fourth Sunday of Lent

JOSHUA 5:9–12; PSALM 34:2–7; 2 CORINTHIANS 5:17–21;
LUKE 15:1–3, 11–32

While the parable of the Prodigal Son can be approached from many angles, at this point in Lent it may be especially helpful to focus on the wayward son and on the dynamic of taking responsibility for one's sins, asking God for forgiveness and being reconciled to God.

The Prodigal Son is a fool and a sinner. He demands his share of his father's estate, goes away and squanders it all. When he is reduced to feeding pigs (in Jewish eyes a deplorable occupation), he finally comes to his senses and determines to take responsibility for his evil actions and to return to his father's household. The Prodigal Son's conduct here is refreshing and unusual. He makes no excuses and does not claim to be a victim. Admitting guilt is the first step toward forgiveness and reconciliation with God.

When he encounters his father, he again admits his sinfulness and foolishness, and is willing to accept the consequences of his bad behavior. The result is reconciliation with his father and restoration to a place of honor in the household. His father is more interested in showing mercy and being reconciled with his son than in administering strict justice. The parable reminds us that we can turn back and receive mercy. We *can* go home again.

Pray

I sought the LORD, and he answered me,
and delivered me from all my fears.
(Psalm 34:4)

Reflect

Is there some area in your life where you need reconciliation with God or someone else? Can you articulate it? Do you want to do something about it now?

The Power of Jesus' Word

March 15 • Monday of the Fourth Week of Lent
ISAIAH 65:17–21; PSALM 30:2, 4–6, 11–13; JOHN 4:43–54

From this point on in Lent most of the Gospel readings for the weekdays are taken from John. Moreover, the focus of the readings shifts from what we can and should do to what God has done and does for us through Jesus' life, death and resurrection.

Today's episode from John—the healing of the official's son—is described as "the second sign that Jesus did" (4:54). There are seven "signs" in John's Gospel. They are miracle stories, with an even deeper function than merely displaying Jesus as an agent of divine power. These signs point toward the "hour" of Jesus, which marks the decisive point in the coming of the "new heavens and a new earth," which in turn will accompany the fullness of God's kingdom (see Isaiah 65:17).

In this second sign a gentile (non-Jewish) official believes that Jesus has the power to heal his son who is near death. One can imagine that every parent in that situation would be willing to try anything. But when Jesus says "your son will live," the official does not go away disappointed (see John 4:50). Rather, he takes Jesus at his word and later finds that the fever left the boy at the exact moment when Jesus said these words.

The sign of the healing of the official's son points to Jesus' revival of Lazarus and to his own resurrection from the dead. It is also a reminder of the power of faith in the word of Jesus.

Pray

Hear, O LORD, and be gracious to me!

O LORD, be my helper! (Psalm 30:10)

Reflect

If your child were near death, how would you feel? What might you do? Would you have taken Jesus at his word?

• • • | • • •

The Third Sign

March 16 • Tuesday of the Fourth Week of Lent
EZEKIEL 47:1–9, 12; PSALM 46:2–3, 5–6, 8–9; JOHN 5:1–16

The third sign performed by Jesus—the healing of a lame man at the pool of Bethzatha in Jerusalem—provides Jesus with the occasion for speeches about his equality with God the Father and the various witnesses to him.

The reading from Ezekiel 47 describes the flowing waters of the New Jerusalem and their life-giving and healing powers. The lame man had kept watch for many years, awaiting a cure. But no cure came until Jesus told him "Stand up, take your mat and walk" (John 5:8). He was healed immediately and completely—at the word of Jesus.

But no good deed goes unpunished. In this case "the Jews" object that by instructing the man to carry his mat, Jesus was in effect commanding him to do work on the Sabbath (John 5:10).

The expression "the Jews" is John's usual way of referring to Jesus' opponents. Of course, it did not include all Jews. And Jesus himself and all his first followers were Jews. The other evangelists tend to distinguish various groups that were hostile to Jesus: scribes, Pharisees, chief priests, elders and so on. Taken out of context, John's usage can foster anti-Jewish sentiments.

In this episode the misunderstanding of Jesus by his opponents (a frequent occurrence in John's Gospel) will offer Jesus the opportunity to explain his somewhat free attitude to Sabbath observance and his identity as the Son of God.

Pray

O God, may you always be my refuge and strength, my everlasting help in distress. Heal me in those areas of my life where I most need healing. Amen.

Reflect

What does the power of Jesus' word suggest about his person? Have you ever found yourself misunderstood and criticized for doing a good deed? How did you react?

• • • | • • •

God as Loving Father and Mother

March 17 • Wednesday of the Fourth Week of Lent
ISAIAH 49:8–15; PSALM 145:8–9, 13–14, 17–18;
JOHN 5:17–30

In response to Jesus' defense of his healing the paralyzed man, his opponents accuse him not only of breaking the Sabbath rest but also of calling God his Father and making himself equal to God. Rather than denying these charges, Jesus affirms his identity as the Son of God and as capable of doing what God does. Indeed, he claims that a perfect unity exists between himself and God as his Father.

Just as a son learns from watching what his father does, so Jesus contends that the Father has given to him the authority to do on the Sabbath what God does: to give life, and to render judgment. For those who believe in Jesus as the revealer and revelation of God, eternal life has already begun. Nevertheless, the fullness of life will come with the resurrection, the last judgment and rewards and punishments.

John's emphasis on God as the father of Jesus and of us all is nicely balanced by the beautiful appeal to a mother's love in today's reading from Isaiah in which God says, "Can a woman forget her nursing child, / or show no compassion for the child of her womb? / Even these may forget, / yet I will not forget you" (49:15). The God revealed in the Bible transcends gender. But we humans need analogies to express our relationship with God. If the Father of our Lord Jesus Christ loves his people with more than any father's or mother's love, should we not love God and one another in response?

Pray

The LORD is near to all who call on him,
to all who call on him in truth.
(Psalm 145:18)

Reflect

What allows Jesus to heal on the Sabbath? Do you believe that eternal life has already begun for you? Do you find the biblical images of God as loving father and mother helpful?

• • • | • • •

Witnesses to Jesus

March 18 • Thursday of the Fourth Week of Lent
Exodus 32:7–14; Psalm 106:19–23; John 5:31–47

Having made extraordinary claims about his authority as the Son of God, Jesus must explain why his claims should be accepted. He first lists various witnesses to him and then criticizes his opponents' unbelief.

Jesus' most important witness is his heavenly Father, the "another" (John 5:32) who testifies for him and the one who sent him to us. A second witness is John the Baptist, described here as "a burning and shining lamp" (5:35). A third witness is the works or signs that Jesus did as part of his mission as the revealer and revelation of God. A fourth witness is Scripture, that is, the Hebrew Bible, or what we call the Old Testament. Instead of searching for eternal life in Scripture, his opponents ought to have turned to him as the Son of God. He is the one to whom Scripture points and the real source of eternal life.

Jesus goes on to reflect on why his opponents have refused to accept him and give their own witness to him. He accuses them of lacking love for God and desiring human praise. And he questions their ability to interpret Scripture. Where they imagine an opposition between Moses and Jesus, there is in fact perfect continuity between them. Jesus warns that rather than defending them, Moses will become their accuser.

Pray
Lord Jesus Christ, you are God's Word and God's Son. May all that I am and do bear witness to you and to your heavenly Father. Amen.

Reflect
Which witness to Jesus is most persuasive for you? How do you witness to Jesus? Why doesn't everyone accept Jesus?

∙ ∙ ∙ | ∙ ∙ ∙

The Troubles of the Just

March 19 • Friday of the Fourth Week of Lent
Wisdom 2:1, 12–22; Psalm 34:17–21, 23;
John 7:1–2, 10, 25–30

It is almost impossible to read today's selection from the book of Wisdom without applying it to Jesus' Passion and death. But that book was written well before Jesus' birth. Today's passage contains echoes from the Servant Songs in Isaiah 40—55 and points forward to Jesus and a whole host of good and righteous persons who have suffered for their fidelity to the gospel and the search for justice.

The just person as described by his enemies in Wisdom 2 is an annoyance because he challenges their customary conduct and claims to be a child of God. Out of envy they want to do away with him and plot to kill him. What they fail to understand is that there is life after death, a divine judgment and eternal life for the righteous: "But the souls of the righteous are in the hand of God" (Wisdom 3:1).

Jesus had opponents also, and they, too, sought to kill him. Yet there was another group, ordinary folk who were curious about Jesus but did not really understand him either. They were impressed enough with Jesus to speculate that he might be the Messiah. But since they knew he was from Nazareth, they were convinced that he could not be the Messiah. However, as readers of John's Gospel know, Jesus was really from his heavenly Father. He was and is the Messiah and much more.

Pray

Lord God, be with those who suffer for their fidelity to you and your commandments. Vindicate them and reward them with eternal life with you. Amen.

Reflect

Why are good persons often unpopular? Can you recall righteous persons of our own time who have been unjustly persecuted and even murdered? Why did this happen?

Joseph as Model of Fidelity

March 19 • Saint Joseph, Husband of the Blessed Virgin Mary
2 Samuel 7:4–5, 12–14, 16; Psalm 89:2–5, 27, 29;
Romans 4:13, 16–18, 22; Matthew 1:16, 18–21, 24
(or Luke 2:41–51)

Today the readings for the Solemnity of Saint Joseph replace those for Friday of the Fourth Week of Lent. In the context of Lent, Joseph exemplifies a central lenten virtue—fidelity. It was through Joseph that Jesus was recognized as a descendant of David and a member of the tribe of Judah. This identity qualified him to be the Messiah of Israel.

In Matthew's Infancy Narrative Joseph is a major figure. Puzzled by Mary's pregnancy, Joseph decides to divorce her quietly rather than expose her to public shame and even death. But like his Old Testament namesake, Joseph is a dreamer. And God communicates with Joseph repeatedly through his dreams. Joseph accepts these dreams as divine communications and faithfully carries out the instructions to take Mary as his wife, to make the child his own, to bring Mary and the child to Egypt for their safety and to return eventually to Nazareth in Galilee.

In his fidelity to God's Word, Joseph stands in the line begun by Abraham, who trusted in God's Word and believed in God's promises despite their apparent impossibility to be fulfilled. In both cases their fidelity was amply rewarded. Their fidelity offers us an important and timely example at this point near the end of Lent.

Pray

Lord God, open my ears and mind to how you speak to me and keep me faithful after the example of Joseph and Abraham. Amen.

Reflect

Imagine yourself in Joseph's position. What would you think? What would you do? What did Joseph contribute to Jesus' identity and formation?

• • • | • • •

Where Did Jesus Come From?

March 20 • Saturday of the Fourth Week of Lent
JEREMIAH 11:18–20; PSALM 7:2–3, 9–12; JOHN 7:40–53

Questions about Jesus' identity and place of origin continue in today's passage from John's Gospel. Some were speculating that Jesus might be a prophet like Moses or even the Messiah. Still others wanted to have Jesus arrested and killed as a dangerous character. Once more Jesus repeats the experience of Jeremiah.

Where Jesus came from is again the topic of debate. Most people in Jerusalem were sure that Jesus came from Nazareth in Galilee. Since the Messiah was to come from Bethlehem in Judah (Micah 5:2–3; Matthew 2:6), they reasoned that Jesus could not be the Messiah. However, they were wrong. In fact, Jesus was born in Bethlehem according to the Infancy Narratives in the Gospels of Matthew and Luke. Moreover, Jesus' real and ultimate origin was from the one whom he called his heavenly Father. He is the man from heaven, the one sent by God to reveal who God is and what God wants to tell us.

John's Gospel is full of misunderstandings and ironies that serve to clarify who Jesus is and where he came from. The Pharisees were certain that they knew all about Jesus. But they were deceived. Those who claimed to know Jesus knew nothing. As readers of John's Gospel, we know how wrong they are. We know that Jesus is not only the Prophet and the Messiah but also the Son of God.

Pray

O LORD my God, in you I take refuge;
   save me from all my pursuers, and deliver me.
   (Psalm 7:1)

Reflect

Who is Jesus for you? Which titles best capture his identity for you? Why did the Pharisees fail to understand him?

• • • | • • •

Three Biblical Themes
March 21 • Fifth Sunday of Lent
ISAIAH 43:16–21; PSALM 126:1–6; PHILIPPIANS 3:8–14;
JOHN 8:1–11

Today's readings can help us connect with three great themes of the Bible: the exodus, the paschal mystery and God's justice and mercy.

The passage from Isaiah 43 was part of the prophet's program to encourage the Jewish exiles in Babylon to return to Jerusalem in the sixth century BC. The exodus from Egypt many centuries before was the pivotal event in ancient Israel's consciousness. By using the imagery of the first exodus, the prophet sets the return from exile in line with that great event of liberation. In both cases the movement is from slavery to freedom.

The term *paschal mystery* describes the saving effects of Jesus' life, death and resurrection. The word *paschal* derives from Passover and so stands alongside the exodus and the return from exile as a major event in the

Christian biblical narrative. How important the paschal mystery was for Paul can be seen from his own words in Philippians. Paul came to regard his past accomplishments in Judaism as "rubbish" (3:8) and wanted only to be "like" (3:10) to Jesus in his death and Resurrection to live out of his saving power.

In dealing with the case of a woman caught in adultery, Jesus displays God's mercy in saving her life and God's justice in not excusing her sin or those of her accusers.

Pray
Restore our fortunes, O LORD,
    like the watercourses in the Negeb.
May those who sow in tears
    reap with shouts of joy. (Psalm 126:4–5)

Reflect
How do these three themes fit together? What do they tell us about the God of the Bible? In what ways do they promote hope?

· · · | · · ·

False Witnesses and True Witnesses

March 22 • Monday of the Fifth Week of Lent
Daniel 13:1–9, 15–17, 19–30, 33–62; Psalm 23:1–6;
John 8:12–20

Today's very long reading from the book of Daniel concerns the false witness made by two elders who were also judges. When Susanna refuses to have sexual relations with them, they make up a story according to which they observed her committing adultery with "a young man" (13:21). Facing shame and even death, Susanna can only pray that their false testimony might be exposed for what it is. In what is sometimes called the first detective story, Daniel interrogates the two elders separately, finds discrepancies between their stories, charges them with perjury and has them executed. Thus the truth comes out, and an innocent woman is vindicated in the face of false witnesses.

When Jesus proclaims himself to be the light of the world, the Pharisees object that he is bearing witness to himself. In response Jesus asserts that his true witness is his heavenly Father, the one who sent him into our world.

In the background of this dispute is the Jewish practice of needing the testimony of two or more witnesses to establish a legal fact (Deuteronomy 17:6; 19:15).

In the case of Jesus his two witnesses are the best and most reliable of all: Jesus, the Son of God, and his heavenly Father. In what is an apt summary of John's Gospel as a whole, Jesus says, "If you knew me, you would know my Father also" (8:19). We come to know the Father in and through Jesus.

Pray
Lord God, may my witness to you always be true and sincere. May you lead me in the way of honesty and guide me in right paths. Amen.

Reflect
What should a witness do in a courtroom? Why is the conduct of the two elders in Daniel 13 so bad? How do you bear witness to Jesus and his Father?

The Lifting of Jesus

March 23 • Tuesday of the Fifth Week of Lent

NUMBERS 21:4–9; PSALM 102:2–3, 16–21; JOHN 8:21–30

As the dialogue with the Pharisees continues, Jesus announces that he is going away to a place where they cannot come—to his heavenly Father. Their misunderstanding provides the occasion for Jesus to explain the difference between them and him. They are from below, while he is from above. They belong to "this world," but he does not (see John 8:23). That is why they fail to believe that Jesus is "I AM," a title applied to God in the Old Testament (Exodus 3:14; Isaiah 43:10–12).

When the opponents ask, "Who are you?" (John 8:25). Jesus explains that they will understand his true identity only when he is "lifted up" (8:28). There is a play on words here, a typical Johannine literary practice. In the Passion Narrative Jesus will be "lifted up" on the cross to die. But his death will set off the sequence of events in which Jesus will be raised from the dead, show himself to his disciples as alive again and be exalted ("lifted up") once more to his heavenly Father.

The strange episode of the bronze serpent in Numbers 21 adds depth to the theme of Jesus being lifted up. When Moses mounted the bronze serpent on a pole, those who had been bitten by serpents and looked upon the bronze serpent were miraculously healed. Likewise, when Jesus is lifted up on the cross, those needing spiritual healing will be able to find it in him and come to recognize that he is "I AM."

Pray

Lord Jesus Christ, as we draw closer to the central mystery of our Christian religion, deepen our faith and give us the eyes to see the significance of the events of Holy Week for us and for our world. Amen.

Reflect

Why did Jesus die? How do you interpret Jesus' death on the cross? How does it relate to our salvation?

$$\cdots \mid \cdots$$

The True Children of Abraham

March 24 • Wednesday of the Fifth Week of Lent
Daniel 3:14–20, 91–92, 95; 52–56; John 8:31–42

When Jesus promises knowledge of the truth and freedom to those who remain in his word, the opponents object that as children of Abraham they have never been slaves. Note that here the dialogue partners are identified as "the Jews who had believed in him" (John 8:31). As the conversation develops, however, it appears that Jesus' claims about himself became too much even for them to accept.

The opponents interpret Jesus' talk about freedom in a political sense. But Jesus is really talking about spiritual slavery and spiritual freedom, "everyone who commits sin is a slave to sin" (8:34). To clarify his role as the Son of God in freeing people from the slavery of sin, Jesus alludes to the process by which slaves in a household might be freed, that is, through the mediation of a son.

When the opponents repeat their claim to be true children of Abraham, Jesus insists that to be children of Abraham they must do the works of Abraham. What made Abraham important is that he heard the Word of

God and acted upon it. The same God who spoke to Abraham now speaks through Jesus as the Word of God. By rejecting his Word, the opponents are showing that they are not true children of Abraham and that God is not their Father. The true children of Abraham serve only the God who spoke through Abraham and speaks through Jesus as the Word of God.

Pray

Blessed are you, O Lord, God of our ancestors,
   and to be praised and highly exalted for ever;
And blessed is your glorious, holy name,
   and to be highly praised and highly exalted forever.
   (Daniel 3:52)

Reflect

How do you understand freedom? Have you ever been a slave to sin? Where or how did you experience your freedom?

· · · | · · ·

Jesus and Abraham

March 25 • Thursday of the Fifth Week of Lent
GENESIS 17:3–9; PSALM 105:4–9; JOHN 8:51–59

According to the book of Genesis, Abraham's greatness consisted in hearing the word of God and believing God's promise that he would become the father of many nations. God's promise to Abraham marked a new step in salvation history after the disastrous beginnings described in Genesis 3—11. And God's covenant with Abraham has shaped the history of the people of God ever since.

According to John's Gospel and the other New Testament books, the Incarnation of Jesus as the Word of God marked another, even greater step. In a new and definitive way Jesus has revealed who God is and what God wants us to know and do. When his opponents protest that by making such high claims about himself Jesus was making himself greater than Abraham, they are ironically correct. The basis for Jesus' claim is his close relationship with God as his Father, "I do know him and I keep his word" (John 8:55).

When Jesus claims Abraham's approval, the opponents deny that he could have had any relationship with Abraham since he is under fifty years of age and Abraham lived many hundreds of years before. The last straw for them comes when Jesus says, "before Abraham was, I am" (John 8:58). Regarding such a statement to be blasphemy (see Leviticus 24:16), the opponents try to stone him.

Pray

Lord God, you have spoken to Abraham and through Jesus. May we listen to your voice in Scripture and in our everyday lives. Amen.

Reflect

How are Abraham and Jesus similar? How do they differ?

• • • | • • •

Mary as Hearer of God's Word

March 25 • The Annunciation of the Lord
ISAIAH 7:10–14; 8:10; PSALM 40:7–11;
HEBREWS 10:4–10; LUKE 1:26–38

Today the readings for the Solemnity of the Annunciation of the Lord replace the readings for the Thursday of the

Fifth Week of Lent. One way to understand today's passage from Luke 1 is to consider it the announcement of Jesus' birth to Mary and so the beginning of the Incarnation of Jesus the Word of God (see John 1:14). The Word becoming flesh (the meaning of *incarnation*) was the necessary precondition for the events that we celebrate during Holy Week.

Mary is a major figure in Luke's Infancy Narrative. In the episode of the Annunciation described in Luke 1, Mary seems to struggle to understand and accept what is being asked of her—to become the mother of the Messiah and the Son of God and to undergo his conception through the agency of the Holy Spirit.

In response to the angel's proposal, Mary summons up the courage to identify herself as the "servant" (or slave) of the Lord and agrees, "let it be with me according to your word" (Luke 1:38). Throughout Luke's Gospel and Acts, Mary fulfills perfectly the role of the ideal disciple as one who hears the word of God and acts upon it (see Luke 8:21; 11:28). As we enter the final days of Lent, may we follow Mary's example by trying to understand God's word and will for us and to act upon it.

Pray

…Here I am;

…

I delight to do your will, O my God.

(Psalm 40:7, 8)

Reflect

Imagine yourself in Mary's position. What would have been your initial reaction to the angel's proposal? What might have convinced you to say "Yes"?

• • • | • • •

Terror on Every Side

March 26 • Friday of the Fifth Week of Lent
Jeremiah 20:10–13; Psalm 18:2–7; John 10:31–42

We sometimes imagine that the great characters of the Bible lived peaceful and worry-free lives. Today's Scripture readings prove that assumption wrong. Jeremiah, the psalmist, and Jesus experienced "Terror… all around!" (Jeremiah 20:10). What sustained them was their trust in God's power to deliver them.

Jeremiah tried unsuccessfully to convince his people that only a religious and spiritual renewal could save Judah from defeat and conquest by the Babylonians. For his efforts he gained many enemies and threats against his life. What sustained Jeremiah was his conviction that the Lord God was his "dread warrior" (20:11).

Likewise, Psalm 18 contains vivid descriptions of some kind of near-death experience. Whether the psalmist was in danger of drowning or merely used that imagery to describe his plight is not clear. What is clear is that in his experience of terror on every side the psalmist called upon God to be his rock, fortress and deliverer.

In today's passage from John 10, Jesus is on the verge of being stoned to death. The opponents charged that "you, though only a human being, are making yourself God" (John 10:33). The irony is that from the Johannine perspective the opponents were correct. Jesus is both human and divine. However, in the opponents' eyes such talk was blasphemy. What sustained Jesus was his conviction that "the Father is in me and I am in the Father" (v. 38).

Pray

I love you, O LORD, my strength.

The LORD is my rock, my fortress, and my deliverer. (Psalm 18:1–2)

Reflect

Have you ever experienced "terror...all around"? How did you react? What got you through it?

· · · | · · ·

The Supreme Irony

March 27 • Saturday of the Fifth Week of Lent
Ezekiel 37:21–28; Jeremiah 31:10–13; John 11:45–56

Irony takes place when the reader or listener grasps the true meaning that somehow eludes the speaker. John's Gospel is full of ironies. At the meeting of the Jewish leaders concerning what they should do about Jesus, the high priest Caiaphas says that "it is better for you to have one man die for the people than to have the whole nation destroyed" (John 11:50). This is the supreme irony.

Caiaphas and his companions probably had an ideal view of Israel, something like what is described in Ezekiel 37. There the sixth-century BC prophet looked forward to Israel having returned from exile, united under one Davidic prince, cleansed from sin, living peacefully in the Promised Land, with God dwelling in the Jerusalem temple and worshipped by all the other nations.

This hope was not a reality in Jesus' time. Rather, Israel was a small part of the Roman Empire. The chief priest and his allies regarded Jesus as a possible threat to the relative peace they had managed to negotiate with the Romans. From a pragmatic political viewpoint it was better that one troublemaker should be executed if that would help to keep the peace. But the Romans did destroy Jerusalem and its temple in AD 70. The irony was Jesus was to die not only for his nation but for all the peoples of the world. Thus Caiaphas was a prophet in spite of himself. This was the supreme irony.

Pray

Lord God, as we approach Holy Week, help us to see your hand at work in the events that we commemorate and to grasp their significance for all of humankind. Amen.

Reflect

Why did the Jewish leaders regard Jesus as dangerous? In what sense was Caiaphas a prophet? Why is Jesus' death significant?

· · · | · · ·

Jesus Exemplifies His Own Teachings

March 28 · Palm Sunday of the Lord's Passion
ISAIAH 50:4–7; PSALM 22:8–9, 17-20, 23–24; PHILIPPIANS 2:6–11; LUKE 22:14—23:56

The "Seven Last Words of Jesus" are a compilation of sayings attributed to Jesus at the moment of his death in all four Gospels. Three of these sayings are contained in

Luke's Gospel and show Jesus to be the best example of his own teachings.

"Father, forgive them; for they do not know what they are doing" (Luke 23:34). Jesus says these words about those who were crucifying him and the bystanders who were mocking him. Throughout Luke's Gospel, Jesus taught about God's willingness to forgive sinners and our obligation to forgive others if we expect to be forgiven by God. He also challenged his followers to love their enemies.

"Today you will be with me in Paradise" (Luke 23:43). Throughout Luke's Gospel, Jesus exercises a ministry of outreach to tax collectors, sinners and other marginalized persons. At the moment of his death, he reaches out to the "good thief" and promises him a place in God's kingdom.

"Father, into your hands I commend my spirit" (Luke 23:46). Here Jesus makes his own the words of Psalm 31:5. Throughout Luke's Gospel, Jesus urged his followers to put their trust and hope in God and rely on God's mercy. Now Jesus practices what he preached as he hangs on the cross, and in trust and hope he awaits his vindication at Easter.

Pray

But you, O LORD, do not be far away!

   O my help, come quickly to my aid!

   (Psalm 22:19).

Reflect

Do you find it hard to forgive those who have harmed you? Do you find it hard to trust God when you are afraid? Where does Jesus' example most challenge you?

• • • | • • •

An Extravagant Anointing
March 29 • Monday of Holy Week
ISAIAH 42:1–7; PSALM 27:1–3, 13–14; JOHN 12:1–11

The Old Testament readings from Monday, Tuesday, Wednesday and Friday during Holy Week are the four "Servant Songs" in Isaiah 40—55. While scholars debate about who the sixth-century BC prophet meant in his own time, early Christians identified this figure with Jesus. In Isaiah 42 the Servant is described as chosen by God to bring justice to the nations in a gentle and nonviolent manner.

The episode described in John 12 takes place in Bethany (a village near Jerusalem) shortly before

Passover. The focus of the story is the anointing of Jesus by Mary. Although anointing the head of a guest was not unusual, anointing the feet and using so much ointment that the excess had to be wiped off was.

Mary's gesture was clearly symbolic. She identified Jesus as the Messiah (which means "the anointed one") and pointed toward Jesus' death and burial (where the corpse would be anointed to keep down the stench). She applied the expensive ointment so lavishly that she had to wipe it off with her hair.

Mary's enthusiasm and extravagance contrast with the calculating attitude displayed by Judas. While ostensibly championing the idea of giving alms to the poor, Judas seems also to be rejecting the idea of Jesus as a suffering Messiah. Only John charges Judas with stealing from the common fund.

Pray

I believe that I shall see the goodness of the LORD
   in the land of the living.
Wait for the LORD;
   be strong, and let your heart take courage;
   wait for the LORD! (Psalm 27:13–14)

Reflect

What led early Christians to identify Jesus as the Servant figure in Isaiah 42? Why was Mary of Bethany's extravagant action important? Why was Judas wrong in his reaction?

• • • | • • •

Glory Amid Betrayals

March 30 • Tuesday of Holy Week
ISAIAH 49:1–6; PSALM 71:1–6, 15, 17; JOHN 13:21–33, 36–38

According to Isaiah 49, the Servant of the Lord was chosen from birth to be God's instrument in bringing Israel back to the Lord and forming his chosen people into a light to the nations. Fulfilling that mission was difficult and seemed to be in vain. But the Servant's reward came from God.

Today's Gospel reading comes from near the beginning of John's narrative of Jesus' Last Supper. It contrasts Judas's betrayal of Jesus and Peter's denial of him with Jesus' own interpretation of what awaits him—that his arrest, trials, crucifixion, death, resurrection and exaltation will be his hour of glory.

The betrayals are shocking. Judas had been among Jesus' inner circle. He had seen and heard Jesus for a long period. As the community treasurer, he played an important role among the twelve. Likewise, Peter is always listed first among the twelve, often serves as their spokesman and will be the "rock" on which the church will be built.

Between Jesus' prophecies about these shocking betrayals and denials is his own extraordinarily positive perspective on the events of Holy Week. For Jesus, they are not a defeat but rather the moment when he and his heavenly Father are to be glorified. His interpretation challenges us to look at Holy Week from Jesus' own perspective as recorded by John—as his hour of glory.

Pray

For you, O Lord, are my hope,
  my trust, O Lord, from my youth.
Upon you I have leaned from my birth;
  it was you who took me from my mother's womb.
  (Psalm 71:5–6)

Reflect

What aspects of Jesus are foretold by the Servant Song in Isaiah 49? In what sense could Jesus be glorified through the events of Holy Week? How does Jesus' behavior compare with that of his disciples?

• • • | • • •
Why Did Judas Betray Jesus?

March 31 • Wednesday of Holy Week

ISAIAH 50:4–9; PSALM 69:8–10, 21–22, 31, 33–34; MATTHEW 26:14–25

In the Servant Song in Isaiah the theme of the Servant's physical suffering becomes more prominent. The Servant recounts his own punishments endured in carrying out his mission to encourage the exiled people of God. It was his trust in the Lord God as the one who "helps me" that enabled him to remain faithful to his task (see 50:7, 9).

That Judas betrayed Jesus was very embarrassing to early Christians. Nevertheless, they always include him among the twelve apostles and remind us that Judas was the one who "handed over" Jesus. The Gospel accounts generally point to Judas' love of money as a motive. Matthew claims that Judas betrayed Jesus for thirty pieces of silver, the price set as recompense for killing someone's slave. Modern scholars have suggested that Judas was rejecting the idea of a suffering Messiah or hoped to broker a deal between Jesus and the Jewish authorities or sought to set off the chain of events that might bring about the fullness of the kingdom of God.

We will probably never know precisely why Judas did what he did. His negative example warns us that even those who were once very close to Jesus can fall away, with disastrous consequences. On what is sometimes called "Spy Wednesday," let us hope that there is enough of God's mercy to extend even to Judas.

Pray

Lord God, we beg for your mercy and pardon for our sins and those of others who in so many ways have betrayed Jesus. Amen.

Reflect

What in the Third Servant Song illuminates the person of Jesus? Why was Judas' betrayal of Jesus so embarrassing to early Christians? Could God be merciful even to Judas?

• • • | • • •

Jesus' Humble Service

April 1 • Holy Thursday
Exodus 12:1–8, 11–14; Psalm 116:12–13, 15–18; 1 Corinthians 11:23–26; John 13:1–15

According to John, Jesus' Last Supper with his disciples took place some twenty-four hours before the eight-day Passover festival began. The great theme of Passover (Israel's passage from slavery to freedom) and the ritual sacrifice of the Passover lamb provide the background for

Jesus' institution of the Eucharist and his washing of his disciples' feet.

Paul's account is the earliest version of the Eucharist in the New Testament. Jesus identifies the bread as his body and cup of wine as his blood and urges his followers to "Do this in remembrance of me" (1 Corinthians 11:24). This ritual also contains elements of sacrifice and the covenant renewal ceremony.

John's lengthy description of the Last Supper begins with Jesus washing the disciples' feet. This task would normally have been carried out by a slave or servant. In performing it Jesus once more identifies himself as the Servant of the Lord and signifies that what he is about to accomplish in his "hour" is the humble service of others (John 13:1).

In his dialogue with Peter, Jesus insists that his death has great meaning for the disciples, and they must accept his humble service. Thus Peter is challenged to accept the gift of salvation that comes through the humiliation of Jesus' crucifixion. And so are we.

Pray

What shall I return to the LORD
    for all his bounty to me? (Psalm 116:12)

Reflect

How is Jesus' death related to Passover? How do you understand the foot washing? Does it challenge you to undertake humble service for others?

· · · | · · ·

The Community of Compassion

April 2 · Good Friday of the Lord's Passion
Isaiah 52:13–53:12; Psalm 31:2, 6, 12–13, 15–17, 25;
Hebrews 4:14–16; 5:7–9; John 18:1—19:42

The Fourth Servant Song is the one most open to interpretation in terms of Jesus' Passion and death. It describes the Servant's sufferings in graphic detail and introduces the idea of his expiatory or vicarious suffering. That is, his suffering has the effect of wiping away or atoning for the sins of others. This concept provides the theological background to early Christian confessions that Jesus died for us and for our sins.

The atoning value of Jesus' death is the main subject in the Letter to the Hebrews. His death on the cross was the perfect (in the sense of effectiveness) sacrifice for sins. Since in the ancient world priests were the ones who offered sacrifices, Jesus acts as the great high priest by willingly offering himself.

The Passion according to John is always read on Good Friday. The climax occurs at the foot of the cross when Jesus, his mother and the beloved disciple constitute a community of compassion. For any mother to watch her child die is among the most painful of human experiences. At the moment of death, Jesus shows concern for his mother and his disciple. In entrusting them to one another, Jesus creates a community in solidarity with all who suffer. His mission as the Suffering Servant is carried on through the community formed at the cross.

Pray

Into your hand I commit my spirit;

you have redeemed me, O LORD, faithful God.

(Psalm 31:5)

Reflect

Were you there when they crucified your Lord? Why did Jesus die? How do you understand the idea of expiatory or vicarious suffering?

· · · | · · ·

Christ Is Risen!

April 3 • Holy Saturday: The Resurrection of the Lord—Easter Vigil
Genesis 1:1—2:2; Romans 6:3–11; Luke 24:1–12

At the Easter Vigil there are seven Old Testament readings with accompanying Responsorial Psalms, along with two New Testament readings. The Old Testament passages place Jesus' Resurrection in the context of salvation history. The First Readings concern God's creation of the world, Abraham's willingness to sacrifice his son Isaac and the exodus from Egypt.

Luke's account of the empty tomb tells how a group of Jesus' women followers came to his tomb on Easter morning in order to complete the burial rituals. These women saw Jesus die on the cross. They saw his body taken down and placed in a tomb-cave owned by Joseph of Arimathea. When they arrive at the tomb, they find the large stone rolled away from the entrance and the tomb opened and empty. They are informed by "two men in dazzling clothes" that Jesus had been raised from the dead (see Luke 24:4). The women in turn went and told the apostles what they saw and heard.

The significance of Jesus' Resurrection for us is brought out by Paul. Very early in Christian history baptism came to be interpreted in relation to Jesus' death and Resurrection. Water symbolizes both death (immersion into it) and life (emerging out of it). Baptism means dying to sin and living for God. That is why baptism is part of the Easter Vigil.

Pray
Create in me a clean heart, O God,
  and put a new and right spirit within me.
(Psalm 51:10)

Reflect
How do the Old Testament readings help you to appreciate Jesus' Resurrection? What does the empty tomb prove? Why do we renew our baptismal promises at Easter?

· · · | · · ·

Easter—Past, Present and Future

April 4 · Easter Sunday

Acts 10:34, 37–43; Psalm 118:1–2, 16–17, 22–23; Colossians 3:1–4 (or 1 Corinthians 5:6–8); John 20:1–9

The Easter event—Jesus' Resurrection from the dead—occurred almost two thousand years ago. According to John, Mary Magdalene first found Jesus' tomb empty and went and told Peter and the beloved disciple. Those two disciples engage in a kind of foot race and discover the tomb empty and the burial clothes and head covering rolled up in an orderly way. The beloved disciple "saw and believed" (John 20:8). He seems to have intuited that Jesus had been raised from the dead and that the new age and new creation were beginning.

Peter's speech from Acts 10 adds two important elements to our faith in the Resurrection of Jesus. He refers to the many appearances of the Risen Jesus and his commission that the recipients of those appearances should bear witness to him. Moreover, the remarkable change that came over the disciples (Peter had denied Jesus three times) is further proof that something very extraordinary happened on the first Easter Sunday.

The reading from the Letter to the Colossians reminds us that in the present we repeat the Easter experience by our identification with Jesus' death and Resurrection in our baptism. Paul also points to the future by affirming that when Christ appears once more to judge the living and the dead, we, too, will appear with him in glory.

Pray

O give thanks to the LORD, for he is good;
   his steadfast love endures forever! (Psalm 118:1)

Reflect

How do you explain the transformation that occurred among Peter and the other disciples at Easter? Do you believe that your eternal life has begun with your baptism? How might that conviction shape how you live now?